THE TRAVELER'S VADE MECUM

THE
TRAVELER'S
VADE MECUM

Edited by

HELEN KLEIN ROSS

A Poetry Anthology

 Red Hen Press | *Pasadena, CA*

Cover design and book layout by Cassidy Trier

Library of Congress Cataloging-in-Publication Data

Names: Ross, Helen Klein, editor.
Title: The traveler's vade mecum / edited by Helen Klein Ross.
Description: First edition. | Pasadena, CA : Red Hen Press, [2016]
Identifiers: LCCN 2016023198 (print) | LCCN 2016043085 (ebook) | ISBN
    9781597092241 (softcover : acid-free paper) | ISBN 9781597095068
Subjects: LCSH: American poetry—21st century | BISAC: LITERARY
    COLLECTIONS / General.
Classification: LCC PS617 .T73 2016 (print) | LCC PS617 (ebook) | DDC
    811/.608—dc23
LC record available at https://lccn.loc.gov/2016023198

The Los Angeles County Arts Commission, the National Endowment for the Arts, Pasadena Tournament of Roses, the Pasadena Arts & Culture Commission and the City of Pasadena Cultural Affairs Division, the Los Angeles Department of Cultural Affairs, Dwight Stuart Youth Fund, Sony Pictures Entertainment, and the Ahmanson Foundation partially support Red Hen Press.

First Edition
Published by Red Hen Press
www.redhen.org

ACKNOWLEDGMENTS

I am pleased that some of the poems created for this project found homes before this book could be published. I wish to acknowledge the editors and publishers of these publications, and to thank the poets for permission to reprint their work here. "Everything Here Looks Very Dismal" by Ann Fisher-Wirth appeared in *Cave Wall*, 2015. "I Have Discovered an Error" by Anna Rabinowitz appeared in *Caliban #8* and in her book *Words on the Street*, published by Tupelo Press, 2016. "I Start for Home This Day" by Norbert Hirschhorn appeared in his book *Monastery of the Moon*, published by Dar al Jadid, Beirut, 2012. "It Is a Case of Necessity" by Quinn Latimer appeared as "Tongue Pictures" in *Cura No. 17*, 2014. "It Is No Secret Here" by Sandra Beasley appeared in *Agni*, 2012, and in her book *Count the Waves*, published by W. W. Norton, 2015. "Please Give Me the Name Of" by Barry Goldensohn appeared in his book *The Hundred Yard Dash Man: New and Selected Poems*, published by Fomite Press, 2014. "Symptoms Are Unfavorable, And Alarming" by Michael Gottlieb appeared in his book *Dear All*, published by Roof Books, 2013. "The Enterprise is Abandoned" by Frank Bidart appeared in his book *Metaphysical Dog*, published by Farrar, Straus and Giroux, 2013. "The Heirs Will Not Consent" by Michael Tyrell appeared as "Son & Heir" in *Fogged Clarity*, 2014. "The Rain Is Over, Apparently" by Lynn Melnick appeared in her book *If I Should Say I Have Hope*, published by YesYes Books, 2012. "What is the Wholesale Price of The Traveler's Vade Mecum?" by Sandra Beasley appeared in *The Virginia Quarterly Review*, Fall 2012, and in her book *Count the Waves*, published by W. W. Norton, 2015. "Things Do Not Look as Dismal As They Did" by Barbara Ungar appeared in her book *Immortal Medusa*, published by The Word Works, 2015.

First and foremost, I am grateful to the poets who responded to an unprecedented call with an outpouring of generosity, and with uncommon velocity. I'm grateful to those whose work appears herein, and also to poets whose work has been collected for a second volume.

I am grateful to Frank Bidart for ongoing enlightenments and for his early encouragement of this project.

I am grateful to Lucie Brock-Broido who has illuminated infinite paths in poetry for me and for others.

I am grateful to Billy Collins for luring new travelers into poetry and for inspiring me to explore horizons of the art beyond Pear Tree.

I am grateful to David Lehman whose classroom was a refuge for me in fall of 2001 and for his *Best American Poetry* series which provides instructive examples of how an anthologist should approach a collection.

I am grateful to Alan Ziegler whose most recent anthology involved the task of collecting works by hundreds of poets, written over the course of five centuries. His *SHORT: An International Anthology of Five Centuries of Short-Short Stories, Prose Poems, Brief Essays, and Other Short Prose Forms* (Persea Books, 2013) served as a beacon to me, especially in the last weeks of assembling this project.

I am grateful to Valerie Borchardt for her tenacity and to Kate Johnson for her steady guidance in navigating this book through publishing waters.

Infinite gratitude to Red Hen Press for the courage to take on this unconventional project. To Kate Gale, Mark Cull, Alisa Trager, Selena Trager, and Taline Rumaya, multitudinous thanks for your patience, vision, forbearance, and editorial acumen. And to Cassidy Trier for poetic design.

I am forever grateful to Donald, cherished companion in all of my travels.

*In memory of my father, Rudolph J. Klein,
who taught me the code of A. C. Baldwin's
mentor Samuel Morse and like them, was
dedicated to inventing a better world.*

TABLE OF CONTENTS

Incident

Suspension

Post Scriptum

This anthology is based on a remarkable book printed in 1853, entitled *The Traveler's Vade Mecum; or Instantaneous Letter Writer*, which was a compendium of 8,466 numbered sentences created for travelers. Its author, A. C. Baldwin, was a pastor, poet, and pioneering consumer advocate who saw that a whole sentence could be communicated by merely telegraphing its number, thereby saving the traveler time and expense. For instance, "I am on board a steamer ship bound for Paris" could be abbreviated to "45-Paris," provided the recipient of the message owned (and carried) a copy of the reference manual that would contain its translation. Likewise, "4205" would be all it would take to ruin someone's Grand Tour with "Your house is at the present moment on fire."

An original copy of Baldwin's *The Traveler's Vade Mecum* is preserved in the Reference Department of the New York Public Library. It was digitized by Google Books and is available in PDF form to anyone with internet access. I learned about it through Twitter and my first attempt at appropriating it was to make a found poem out of some of its sentences myself. The poem didn't work. It bore nothing of the richness and range contained in the original document; missing was a linguistic complexity that could only be achieved through a multiplicity of voices. This multiplicity, it seemed to me, was essential to Baldwin's book. He tried to imagine all the things—every single thing—that would need to be said by so many people from so many places, urgent questions like "Do You Know Of A Person Going West Soon, Who Would Take A Lady Under His Protection?" (p. 63), news alerts such as "A Sad Accident Has Happened" (p. 78) and benign assurance that one is alive and well, the equivalent of today's status update, "We Abound In Good Cheer" (p. 35). The accuracy of text is remarkable, given that the book was produced before automated means of checking for error. There are a few obvious word omissions, however, that make for better poem titles than communiqués, such as "The Weather Is Fine, And I Am Improving It" (p. 85).

Using communication advances that Baldwin could only dream of, I approached over a hundred poets in November 2011 and asked each to write a poem with a title consisting of a sentence I'd chosen for them from *The Traveler's Vade Mecum*.

Occasionally, I assigned one title to two poets whose work is quite different, to see what each would make of the same prompt. (Beth Baruch Joselow and Tim Cresswell both interpret "It Is Complete," p. 54 and 125.) The response to my call was gratifying, not only in the velocity of response (most of these poems were received within weeks, speed befitting a project based on telegraphic communication) but also in the diversity of voices and styles and forms. Here are lyric poems, L=A=N=G=U=A=G=E poems, prose poems, found poems, haikus, pantoums, ekphrases, epistolatory poems, acrostics, sonnets, and mirror sonnets. This book isn't only an anthology, it's a compendium of poetics.

Contributors include not only well-known poets such as Bollingen Prize winner Frank Bidart, former US Poet Laureate Billy Collins, and *The Best American Poetry* series editor David Lehman, but also poets like Huang Fan whose work is known mainly abroad (in his case, China) as well as stars of a new generation of poets like Sandra Beasley, Denise Duhamel, Emily Fragos, and Eva Hooker. Beasley's enthusiasm and support for this project resulted in her chapbook *None in the Same Room: Poems from the Traveler's Vade Mecum*, winner of the Center for Book Arts 2013 Prize. I am grateful to all poets here for being game to participate in this unusual "crowd-sourced" project.

What readers will discover herein hasn't only to do with poetry. The collective titles from the original *Vade Mecum* (Latin for "go with me") provide a rare and fascinating glimpse into the habits, diction, and social aspects of nineteenth-century America. It is my hope that this "sequel" provides an equal measure of enlightenment on how our culture has evolved.

—*Helen Klein Ross, Editor*

THE TRAVELER'S

VADE MECUM;

OR

INSTANTANEOUS LETTER WRITER,

BY

MAIL OR TELEGRAPH,

FOR THE CONVENIENCE OF PERSONS TRAVELING ON
BUSINESS OR FOR PLEASURE,

AND FOR OTHERS,

WHEREBY A VAST AMOUNT

OF

TIME, LABOR, AND TROUBLE IS SAVED.

BY A. C. BALDWIN.

NEW YORK:
PUBLISHED BY A. S. BARNES AND CO.
CINCINNATI: H. W. DERBY AND CO.   LONDON: SAMP-
SON, LOW AND SON.
1853.

1. BE sure that your correspondent has a copy, or access to one. If necessary, send him, or her, one by mail.

2. Be careful and not mistake the numbers, and write your figures distinct and plain.

3. If there is a blank in the phrase to be filled, or a word in it you wish to change, write the word, or words, in their order on a line with the number. In some cases the substitution of a word may make bad grammar, but if the *idea* is plain, it is of little consequence.

4. Look for synonyms if you do not find at first what you wish.

5. Always keep in your Book a *pencil, cards* with a margin on both sides for numbers, and *gum-sealed envelopes* with postage stamps previously attached, and you will be prepared to write and send your letter in any emergency.

6. If you have a secret communication to make, agree previously with your correspondent upon a certain arithmetical number which you are to use mutually as a *key* to your phrase. This key is to be added or subtracted, as you may agree, to the number sent by Telegraph.

EXAMPLE. Suppose you agree upon + 10 as your key ; you wish to communicate secrectly the phrase, numbered 748, " *I wish you to attack property without delay,*" but you write 738, which has no reference to your business. Your correspondent adds 10, and comes at once to your true meaning.

Another method is, to use letters to represent figures, in the margin.

agreeably surprised to meet on board the cars my old friend, Mrs. Jones, who will accompany me as far as Brookfield. We are honored by having as fellow passenger, a no less distinguished personage than Frank Pierce. I am in one of the patent ventilated cars, which in a good measure excludes the dust, but not entirely.

We are now entering the city of Springfield, at eleven o'clock forty minutes. At this place we shall exchange cars. The scenery on the banks of the river is perfectly enchanting.

Twelve o'clock. We are now on the cars for New York. We are passing through a delightful country, and the prospect is quite exhilarating.

It is now half past one o'clock, and we are at New Haven, which is a beautiful place.

Half past five o'clock. We are entering the city of New York, and I am in as good health as when I left home.

My journey has been sustained with less fatigue than was anticipated. I shall go directly to Judson's hotel. You may expect to hear from me again soon. I have not time to write any more now. Good-by.

Most truly yours.

P. S. Inquire for my parasol which I left at the Tremont House.

All this, and much more by reversing the card, can be done *on the way* ; and however great the haste of the traveler may be, a card can be prepared and dropped into the letter-box of the cars, steamer or Post-office, or sent to the Telegraph station, without the loss of a moment of time. Thus the journal of a day's travel may be on its way home while the traveler, without stopping, continues his lightning speed in the opposite direction.

Persons unaccustomed to writing, and to whom the penning of a few lines is a great burden, will find this book an efficient aid and relief in communicating with their friends.

II. Great economy of time and expense in the use of the Magnetic Telegraph.

As a whole sentence is communicated by merely sending its number, much of the labor of the operator is saved.

Several times the amount of matter that is

6	Boston—New York—7¼, A. M.
9	Springfield.
14	Springfield—11.45.
19	
22	Mr. John Smith—Hartford.
21	Mrs. Jones—Brookfield.
23	Frank Pierce.
30	
41	Springfield—11.40.
44	Springfield.
37	
9	12 o'clk—N. Y.
33	
39	1¼ o'clk—N. Haven.
41	N. Y.—5¼.
109	
74	
63	Judson's.
65	
66	
P. S. 92	Parasol—Tremont House.

This card contains the following, as will be seen by referring to the corresponding numbers of the book.

To-day left Boston for New York at half past seven o'clock in the morning, and am now on the cars for Springfield, at which place, un-less accidentally detained, we shall arrive by eleven o'clock forty-five minutes. I am happy to meet several acquaintances on board, which renders it very pleasant. I have been introduced to Mr. John Smith, who politely takes me under his protection as far as Hartford. I was

TRAVELER'S VADE MECUM.

TRAVELING DEPARTMENT.

NOTES BY THE WAY.

1. * I SEND you by mail a book, a duplicate of which I have with me, whereby I shall be enabled to let you hear from me often with very little trouble.
2. Please to accept of this book, by means of which I hope to have the pleasure of exchanging thoughts with you frequently.
3. † I left home to-day at . . . o'clock.
4. I left home yesterday at . . . . .
5. I left home on the . . . . .
6. To-day left . . . . . for . . . . .
7. Yesterday took my departure from . . . for . . . .
8. Left . . . . . on the . . . . .
9. I am now on the cars for . . . . .
10. I am now on the steamer . . . . . for . . . . .
11. I am now in the stage-coach for . . . . .
12. I am now on my way to . . . . .
13. It is now . . . o'clock, and we have made . . . miles.
14. Unless accidentally detained, we shall arrive at . . . by . . . o'clock.
15. We have been delayed somewhat, and shall not arrive as soon as expected.

---

* The postage on this book any distance not over 3,000 miles, is one cent each ounce.

† The pronouns that occur in this book. may be changed on your card to a *proper name*, or to *he, she, we, they, my, his, her*, &c., if there is danger that your correspondent will mistake the person or persons speaking or spoken of.

URGENT—URGENCY.

8186.   Is the matter *urgent?*
8187.   The case is one of great *urgency.*
8188.   The case is not one of great *urgency.*
8189.   I am very *urgent* about it.
8190.   .... is very *urgent* in the matter.

USE.

8191.   I would be glad to know what is the *use?*
8192.   It is of great *use,* and will appear so.
8193.   It is of no *use* to do any thing about it.
8194.   It is of little or no *use.*

VACANCY.

8195.   Is there any *vacancy* to be filled?
8196.   There is a *vacancy* to be filled.
8197.   There is no *vacancy* to be filled.
8198.   There will be a *vacancy* by and by.
8199.   There will be no *vacancy* at present.

VACATION.

8200.   When is *vacation* in your Institution?
8201.   *Vacation* commences on the ....
8202.   During *vacation* I hope to have the pleasure of seeing you.
8203.   When does your *vacation* close?
8204.   *Vacation* closes on the ....

VADE MECUM.

8205.   Please send by early conveyance .... copies of the Traveler's *Vade Mecum.*
8206.   What is the wholesale price of the Traveler's *Vade Mecum?*
8207.   The wholesale price of the Traveler's *Vade Mecum* is $ ....
8208.   Please send a copy of the Traveler's *Vade Mecum* to .... by mail if no other opportunity presents.
8209.   Have you a copy of the Traveler's *Vade Mecum?* if not, I will send you one.
8210.   If you have not a copy of the Traveler's *Vade Mecum,* please obtain one immediately.

VALIDITY.

8211.   The *validity* of it is disputed.

March 24, 2016

In compiling this collection, I have done my best to remain faithful to A. C. Baldwin's original design. His book was divided into sections organized under headings he deemed most applicable to the messages. ("Look for synonyms if you do not find at first what you wish.") I have reproduced some of those headings here. I have also preceded each poem title with the corresponding number of the sentence found in his edition. I take pleasure in acknowledging my obligation to Mr. Baldwin for the amount of labor he expended in the preparation of his work, which, as he states in its preface, "if foreseen, would have discouraged the Author at outset; and even when half completed, he would have relinquished it had it not been for the strong conviction that it would, if properly executed, prove a great public benefit."

For the convenience of persons traveling on business or for pleasure, and for others, whereby a vast amount of time, labor and trouble is saved.

The work, novel in its character, and occupying an entirely new field, is submitted to the public with a confident belief that it will be found useful.

—A. C. Baldwin, prefacing *The Traveler's Vade Mecum*,
A. S. Barnes and Co., New York 1853

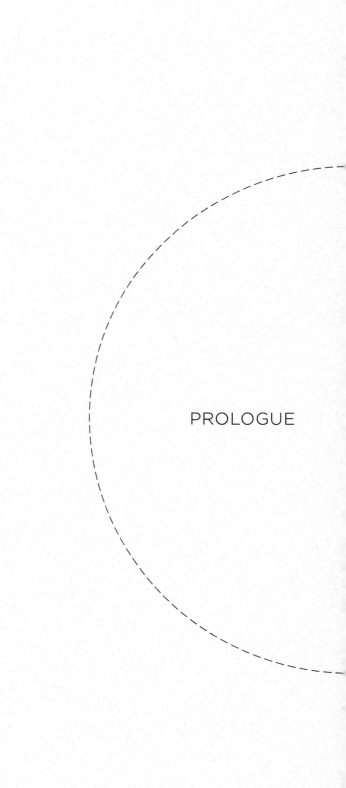

PROLOGUE

4800.

IF HEALTH PERMITS

(Enter Ahab: then, all.)

Read it if you can.
As if it were an anchor.

As if it were a mystic watch.

—*Eva Hooker*

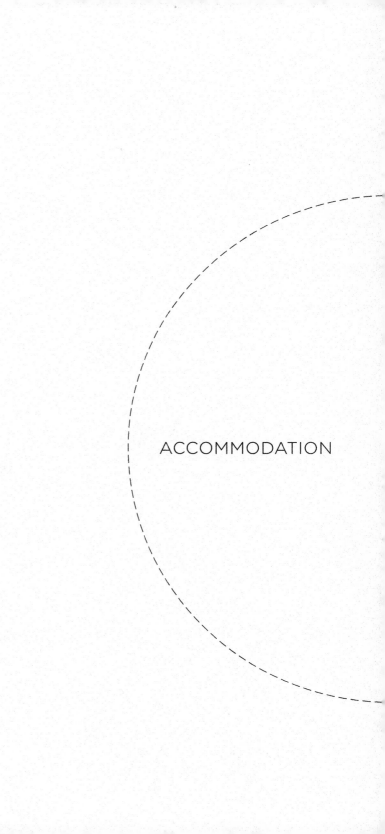

ACCOMMODATION

1573.

THERE WAS A GREAT WANT OF CIVILITY

All night in the trees,
the whispering,
a great disorder, not the way

leaves talk among themselves
during the day, not the rustle
of squirrels and birds among them,

but a tossing, shiftless shadow
weight of darkness,
leaf to leaf.

I dared not close my eyes
for fear it would have
its way with me.

How
could anyone sleep?

—*Julie Suarez*

1723.

OUR FRIENDS HAVE COME

Undersides figgy, sticky
only half-viable:
instars, inchworms, spiderling tarantulas.

Yellow jelly blobs sparkle on a thin rim.

Barbed, fanged, chortling things,
sizeable or hair-thin hooks
snog the skin,

glide their plated geometries in.

—*Lee Gould*

1508.

WE ABOUND IN GOOD CHEER

until the red tide turns deep, and who knows what
lurks underneath to bite our feet clean off.

Some days there are no fish to be had for good money,
and we turn on each other. Even the lovers strain

to say what's best: "Tomorrow the hawks
will circle again against a sky as clear as need."

They will see farther than us, and they will see
scaled ladies bringing bounty to land, to dry dock

and step—even with phantom aches in their hips—
to step with their new shoes into our homes.

—*Erica Wright*

7936.

I SUFFER CONSIDERABLY AT INTERVALS

Darkness enters the room,
the chairs, sofa and bed.

We put our tears in dolly teacups and stir.
I am being elaborate

in the quarters of my attribute
who wears the breast plate of a deity
as her face circles my childhood.

She is lone as the soft spot behind a babe's head.

She lopes and howls and skateboards.
I am all hers and she is mine.

I only tolerate animals—
the human-shaped are not kind.

I have visited homes at dinnertime,
children gathered around the table,
and I have not been content.

As when I am with the man I am a jewel
withheld, anthropomorphic.

No, I will not relinquish my relic.

—*Desirée Alvarez*

179.

I START FOR HOME THIS DAY

Except, *this day* beggars belief
When its proper name is *that day.*

Except, *home* implies a beckoning
When all that remains is a crater.

Except, *start* unleashes release from
Stasis—a sudden fright, flight.

Except, *I* exists only in the
Moment one writes, *I*—
                              I, I, I.

—*Norbert Hirschhorn*

129.

I AM AGREEABLY DISAPPOINTED IN THIS PLACE

How many brothers are planted in this world?
Calf jackets and axe handles, in the land that wasn't their father's.

Onion and amethysts in the petrified mud.
The exile enters, embattled old wolf. Forget the bristling thicket.

Wander over scorched black earth because today's project
is not the sniffing of rodent ribs, not these pickings

in the twigs. Nor is he. Skeletons dedicate poems
to all the bones in this world. And they ought to,

understanding death. The nearly forgotten snow becomes critical.
The life of any March ghost is a search for peace.

Take a head-flash that takes the night into itself:
Hare-flocked moon, smoking past husks. Hacked up on your own

lost ground, some thoughts depend on who you are once you're gone.

—*Stephen Massimilla*

3021.

I HAVE DISCOVERED AN ERROR

Who is the criminal?
In whose custody is the property?

Disobeyed instructions in complete disorder . . .
The object I fear can never be accomplished

Do not travel in the night if you can possibly avoid it
Much that was previously deposited has been withdrawn

The democracy has been defeated

    Love to the baby and a kiss for everyone

The affairs of the crops are in a critical state,
Unpromising, almost a failure
And the prospect through which we are passing
    Is quite indifferent

    What is the answer?   *What* is the answer?

Many of the passengers are sick
Currency is deranged

Clouds are flying away,
      defrauded in the transaction

The roads are dry; the streams are dry
The tide is down
Business is down
Exchange is down
Wages are down and workmen are plenty

You are hereby dismissed from my employment

Love to the baby and a kiss for everyone

—Anna Rabinowitz

1516.

THE CHILDREN WISH TO BE AFFECTIONATELY REMEMBERED

As is proper, their right, their due
only I no longer remember their names
or those of their children
or how many there are
and how they suffered from one thing and another
although I did once.
Where do they live now?

I remember where my dogs are buried
and I remember to water the plants that grow
on their graves. Harry went first, lying in front of the fire.
A weeping cherry grows nearby.
Rosie went next, my favorite. I knew death was coming
and all day we waited, her in my arms,
near the end she made a terrible human groaning,
I don't think it was pain or fear,
she was enduring this next thing,
and I held her and held her
and when it was done I was old.
The children appeared and planted a rose tree.
I remember all of Dover Beach
and Steve Buscemi's name and two of the movies
he starred in: Fargo and Con Air.
Funny.
And I remember the recipe for icing.

—Abigail Thomas

8369.

MY WIFE UNITES WITH ME IN KIND REGARDS

My wife unites with me in kind regards.
About everything else we disagree.

—*Chip Brown*

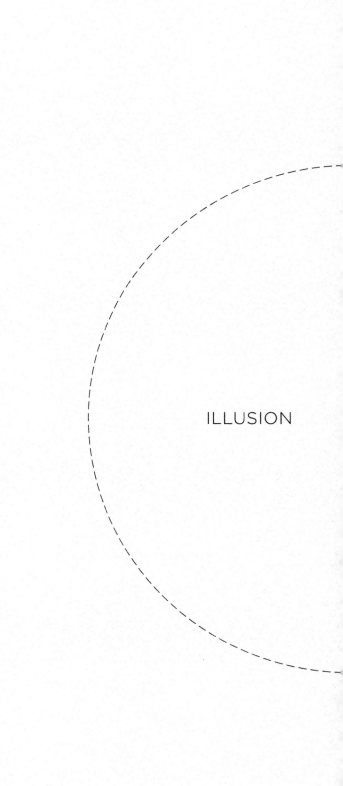

ILLUSION

49.

THE CLOUDS LOOK THREATENING,
AND THERE'S THE PROSPECT OF A STORM

The clouds look threatening, and there's the prospect of a storm
The moon's a white crescent in a blue indifferent sky
Green the evening, the autumn air is warm
And dry, so we sip our drinks and get high,
For we are in Provence and I'm your gendarme
Let's play two truths and a lie
Okay name a beautiful woman who has no arms
That's too easy it's at the Louvre her name is Venus
Are you six feet one do you weigh one eighty five
Yes but ten of those pounds are pure penis
(To paraphrase Ava Gardner) What I mean is
How lucky to be alive
On this November day in 2011
One day nearer to heaven

—*David Lehman*

2469.

One night with nothing to do
I caught her in the garden.
She claimed to have once been
Daughter of Burning Duchess.
We stared at the stars for a while. Life
Had disappointed us, and so to her,
I was a spirit disembodied,
She herself a similar freak.
Before she left for good,
She gave herself one last time
To the old gardener who had crawled
Through a hole in the moon.
Remember, she said, It's my birthday, too.
Take what I've kept from you all these years
Shining in the hell of your hand.
As for me, I still lay my coins down
Just to sleep in the shadows
Of the old town church. Oh hot pursuing fiends!
The dimness, the wreath. No one knows.

—*Richard Stull*

1678.

THE WEATHER IS VERY COLD

The arcade paranoiac hoists a trophy of pulled-out
    roots above his feverish head.
The shaved monkey braves hunger and the wind

    for the gloved hand's stroke.
A child performer in his starched white shirt
    hacks at the strings of a frozen mandolin.

Bald Athena, shivering psychic, has a tooth that needs
    pulling and hammer toes in soft slippers.
She stows her crown and files her nails grown wild.

—Emily Fragos

450.

THE OFFER IS ACCEPTED

              —at crossroads
the signing
         witnessed by the noon
reaper who called the price high but
the sky had been so crowded of late
(balloons traversing the gibbous
moon) I could not imagine
resting there
         so I traded
away the gossamer thing—done
with sound and smoke and promised
soon to work again—
        be assured
your Faust is well now his path
lit by the pitchman

—Ann Aspell

5714.

I HAVE A KEY TO UNLOCK THE WHOLE DIFFICULTY

It is a round stone that codes
mnemonic changes of the dial
across the empty spaces we navigate
inside nursery rhymes and memory
that always seem to track the dead and dying.

The locksmith am I: the trickery
of the fox; the damsel in disguise;
pigs in a house made of sticks; a poison
red apple. What can a child expect?
They don't all believe everything they are told
just before sleep by parents and babysitters.

Some make up their own lies.

—*Monica A. Hand*

7910.

THE STORM IS VIOLENT,
AND DOING MUCH DAMAGE
for Mac Wellman

What are we;

What what what are we;

What are what we;

What we;

Are what we;

Are what, we:

Are we?

What we are!

Are in the sense of are:

Which are we;

Which which which what;

Which of which we are we;

Which we;

Which is which;

Which are which:

Which which?

Which we are?

Are in the sense of are . . .

—*James Sherry*

274.

I SHAN'T TELL YOU WHAT IT IS,
BUT WILL SHOW IT TO YOU WHEN YOU COME

> Elba winched a musty hymnal cube
> twisted to match subtle wine while
> wily beach music bylaws stamina
> Emily's wan Bluet's claim.
>
> That man's twitchy alchemy winches
> twenty mystic bushes and torments
> witches' ascent at thumbs end to
>
> win chattel.
>   I shan't tell you what it is,
> but will show it to you when you come—
> Maybe swab lunch on chutney milt
> and mitten to abett McNulty's wish.

—*Sonja Greckol*

8015.

SYMPTOMS ARE UNFAVORABLE, AND ALARMING

The star-crossed triumphalist

takes his temperature

we are all in violent agreement

that is in no small part

what led to us ending up here

don't get me wrong—

I'm so very good

at doing that

all by myself

—*Michael Gottlieb*

1878.

IT IS COMPLETE

After the hat a rabbit
is a rabbit

no matter
what—

is in itself
complete

and will be as before
undone again

in the ache and chafe
of daily living

tucked away in a paper cabinet
of keepsakes

no matter sprawled
across the margins

where we're
temporarily safe

the Dust Bowl part
of history

maps

the gryphon
yet to appear

—*Beth Baruch Joselow*

1353.

IT IS A CASE OF NECESSITY

That we take hold of the edge—orange-bright

As the tongue touching the knife—

And pull it closer. It edges away, as edges do.

O tacit, O implicit, the holes bespeak

The volumes: the sky.

Bespoke as the case of you: the field

Edged by highway and waterway

And mineral, where we do drink

You. The artist said: *I liked it*

Because it had no subject. The critic liked it

Because without a subject he could not

Criticize it. In some future present,

Foreign moons nod their heavy heads,

Continue their lucid grooming.

Later the sun in august argument

Between you, debating the gods of childhood

And adulthood, and how the whiplash

Of memory (*so edgy*) and its slim sister,

Meaning, might best

Betray you.

—*Quinn Latimer*

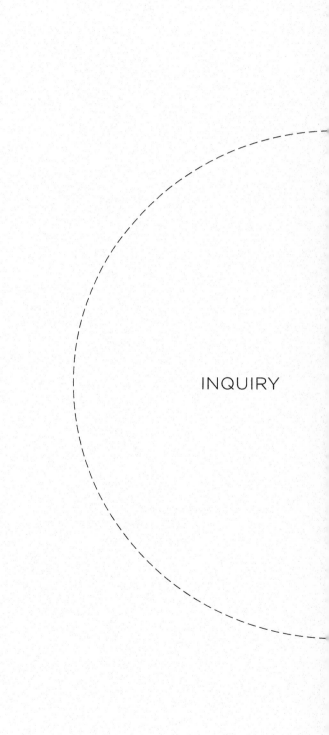

INQUIRY

8206.

WHAT IS THE WHOLESALE PRICE
OF THE TRAVELER'S VADE MECUM?

I intend to converse with many. None in the same room.
I have a daughter to search for, an acre of farmland to sell.
I must confirm that flour is falling and copper is rising;
I must offer my compliments to the ladies.
I will be refusing all medical advice, except for that
of gentlemen known for their punctuality. Where can I find you
in this city? In this parish? In this gypsy market with dirt floors?

If some think me babbling, imagine how a game of chess
appears to one who has only ever known a checkerboard.

I own one suit for going South and another for going under.
I traveled before I was born, and will travel after I die.
They will come together, each clutching their copies,
and raid my library. Beside *Your love is reciprocated,*
they will find four tick marks. Beside *I am fond of loneliness,*
they will find fifteen. A wrought-iron gate makes beautiful
not its bars, but the spaces between its bars. Without structure

there can be no mystery. Dear sirs, thank you for this service.
You have shaken down the Garden of Eden for its seeds.

—Sandra Beasley

8243.

I HAVE A VIVID RECOLLECTION OF IT

How long has it been? Thirty-six years? Not a word from you till now. I often think about—well, I often think. And one thought leads to another. The radio just blared *Jeremiah was a bullfrog*, and I flash to Old Testament prophets, then I'm in Hebrew School, in the hall, telling Beth Gurfein I think she's pretty—before I run away embarrassed.

Do you know I can relive our whole, long-ago summer? The motel on the Cape, the old waitress at the luncheonette, our competing interpretations of *Ulysses*, the long drive home.

I have a vivid recollection of it.

I keep it in a gilt box in a locked drawer in a tiny cubicle in my brain. We're on that long drive home. I'm giving you my standard excuses for breaking up: want to date others, not comfortable in a "couple situation," need my freedom, just not ready. You're silent, but I sense you're crying. I keep my eyes fixed on the road.

Thirty-six years, and it still pulses, glows, pains me when my thoughts touch it. Now here we are late at night, communing on Facebook. You, in a grey world of husband and job; me, still making excuses. We start recalling our Greatest Hits. Song lyrics we both misheard: *You don't have to say you love me, just because of ham*. Laughing at Long Island accents: Hullo? Iz Valerie theh? That black cat, perched on the roof of my car after we saw *The Omen*, and me, screaming, too scared to drive home. A bad omen for us, but the next morning we laughed at the memory. That's the thing. We always laughed.

I have a vivid recollection of it.

—Jimmy Roberts

8328.

DO YOU KNOW OF A PERSON GOING WEST SOON,
WHO WOULD TAKE A LADY UNDER HIS PROTECTION?

Do you know of any sky I might

find the evening spread out against me, picked up all the colors of the day

I've grown tired of this eastern reflection

these avenues mirrored

in the spectacle glass of old men

dug inward

to a place like cement

The women are oddly better at it—resignation

be it a peace that comes with aging

or a secret baked under their lattice crust

Do you know of a person going west soon who doesn't like pie?

—Bergen Hutaff

8254.

HOW LONG SHALL I WAIT?

The hard candy you licked
and ran across my skin.

Jug of vodka—remedy for memory.

The money I have earned and spent.
What good is God in a factory?

Icons, stones, traps.

The faces of our children's children.

The man you left me for. Are we both
waiting for him to die?

How long shall I wait?

—*Laura Cronk*

8288.

HAVE YOU PLENTY OF WATER?

Candles? Firewood?
Old mattresses to lay out on the floor?
A baseball bat in the corner near the door?

Hot dogs, peanut butter, cheerios?
The outline of a hand painted
on the outer wall?

Remember to stash
a notebook or two
in the old van.

Sunshine and footsteps
in the labyrinth
of empty halls.

Alex says sometimes
the farmer's white horse
wanders onto the front

porch. This is where his father
committed suicide. All 350
acres, the empty house, for sale.

—J. Gerard Chalmers

7413.

A REPLY IS NOT NECESSARY

But if I don't respond
how will you know
I received your message?
What if the fax jammed?
What if your email slipped into my spam?
What if I have moved
and the new tenant has thrown
your letter, unopened, into the trash?
Worse—what if she tore the envelope
and recited your correspondence
in a fake British accent
to all of her friends? Don't you want
to be sure that I and only I
have read what you had to say?
Please let me know you still love me.
Please let me know right away.

—*Denise Duhamel*

1412.

IS THERE A CERTAINTY OF IT?

Then I'll be the mother of the waiting room,
Every *no* will rejoin its *yes*,
Every nipple hold the lips that once held it.
I'll be the water, I'll be the child too,
I'll be the tyrant of bandages, keeper of salves,
Every knife will remember its wound.
I'll be paste and tape.
Is there a certainty of it?
The tattoo will reclaim the prisoner's arm.
I'll be the black oak's shade,
I'll be a door to its comings and goings,
the hook holding the still quiet of it.

—*Abigail Wender*

80.

SOME OF THE PASSENGERS WERE KILLED
BY THE ACCIDENT

Rain has laid the dust.

It is feared we will be overcome

By a great array of beauty.

I am fond of loneliness.

Penning a few lines is a burden.

Can you preach for me?

Either grave or ludicrous.

For my pulpit. My parasol.

Through a dismal country,

Ice is making very fast.

Cars run off the track.

Blow. Blood. Blame.

The bodies have all been removed.

Abandon. Alarm. Apology.

Have you seen my daughter?

—*Jo Sarzotti*

2429.

She's glad this day the birds are gone away
With songs that are no longer songs in fields
That are no longer farms. Without the one,
The young whose hand held hers up hills of green
To rest, to roll, to find the clement end
In earth now scorched and scorned by spite, by grief.
Sky clear, severe — the blue above the brown.

—*Catherine Woodard*

483.

HAVE YOU ACCOMPLISHED YOUR OBJECT?

You were at a café, a cup of thick, delicious chocolate at hand.
You drank it all.

No, not all. One taste remained . . . not dregs, no: last
but not least.

"¿Listo?" The waiter breezed by, snatched the cup before
you had a chance to answer.

Did you call him back, smirk self-slightingly, confess
to wanting even the last drops?

Or did your body lunge in the throes of sudden deprivation?
a yelp drawing his attention.

Either way you'd have prevailed: the cup and its sweet
residue again at your beck.

Did you bear the loss as fate? martyred anew by life's
copious misadventure. Gathered up

what was left you, staggered toward the door, the shadow
of your sorrows lengthening

always more . . . No, you cherished the loss. In your mind's eye
it shines: the latest holy grail.

—*Gregg Friedberg*

8428.

I HAVE WRITTEN SEVERAL TIMES, BUT GET
NO ANSWER; WHAT CAN BE THE REASON?

Did you ever live here?
Play Bach Inventions,
my grandchild

conducting from her high chair?
Did we cook vegetarian?
Give puppet shows for Faye

even when you moved away
but not so far as now—
almost Cuba

with your Cuban?
Were you ever
married to my son?

I sent Faye butterflies,
did they come?
Tell me, Catherine,

is your daughter fat?

—Ann Settel

3630.

Have I said too much already?
If I do, you can cut me off.
Texting keeps me steady.
Say when it is enough.

You may have cut me off.
I'll wait, and try again.
Say when it is enough.
I'll ping you from the train.

Is it too soon to talk again?
I know I tend to talk too much.
I'll beep you from the train.
I have a fear of losing touch.

When I start to talk too much
I sense you start to suffocate.
I have a fear of losing touch.
Your messages arrive too late.

You have begun to suffocate,
But texting keeps me steady.

Your messages arrive too late.
I have said too much already.

—*David M. Katz*

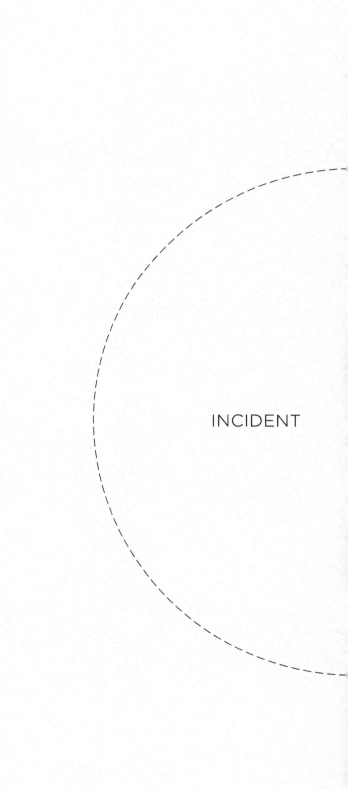

INCIDENT

7777.

THERE ARE SIGNS OF A GALE

Spring is tired, a gale is coming,
fallen leaves start to make their way home,
they're wheels in the wind, no brakes can stop them.
Are they fleeing these awful high-rises?

I go silent, watching leaves spin gleefully
like they've found love.
I see clouds crane their necks towards the water's mirror.
Only fish don't blink, studying and studying
thunder in the dark clouds' heart.

And the sky is a happy backpacker
carrying black clouds
loaded with secrets whistled by the gale.
Paper scraps on the street spin into mice
shuddering at the clouds' black cats.

Ship after ship, like bride after bride.
One by one, they retreat to the port's boudoir
and refuse to marry.
When the gale finally comes
what it tosses so ruthlessly isn't the sea,
it's the fate of those on the water.

—*Huang Fan*
translated by Margaret Ross

461.

A SAD ACCIDENT HAS HAPPENED

on the tightrope strung between
bridge and bridge where
she Walked over the winter water
not yet frozen where she Carried
the balancing stick where she Saw
a city joined to another city
at such height, the tiny windows
high rising, lit or unlit, facing
one another and their promise
of lovely offices so that even un-kept
the last word before the falling
she Spoke in the language of marvel.

—*Gail Segal*

1019.

THE BODY HAS BEEN FOUND

For immediate release: Finally. Whatever fleshes up
devoid of cartilage and desire from the ditch
of the ancients is not for law to rake
and ruin. The normal body is lose-lose, a case
we're drowsing through on a screen
we can't afford. Oh, look, that assassination
is looped. Sorry for the interruption. Parental advisory:
the following images are graphic and may be
permanently enlightening at the subcutaneous
level. At the scene: difference and slough,
cakes and ale, all the cells replaced *moderato*,
praise be. Interpret the evidence: in the upper left
of this mural scratched into the motel wall
an empty preacher (unconfirmed)
appears above a hanging female tongue reaching
joint-like to the knees where—according to eyewitnesses
spokespeople agents more unconfirmed reports
prophets gasbags deputy counselors nuns and
unnamed sources too close for comfort who speak
only on condition of distance—the soul attaches.
These pages have learned that authorities
suspect the alleged subject has been lost
two thousand years and more. That doesn't mean
the corpse is Christy or this shroud doesn't make
its or your ass look bony as *Rocinante*. Check your listings
for services. Flowers and grievances can be sent

to survivors of choice. Now please step back
and let us weigh the soul of this dead dog.

—*Harry Bauld*

73.

THE JOURNEY WAS NOT AS PLEASANT
AS ANTICIPATED

The hero wasn't in the mood to leave home
and the dull rain delayed us in St. Louis.

I woke up late and left my book at home,
then we hit an iceberg and had to evacuate.

A flock of wild terrorists got caught in the engine,
but the pilot was an ace and made a textbook landing.

The bar was out of gin and our deck was short an ace.
A desperate man's life derailed the train.

Emma was seasick all day on the deck,
then ran into the man who broke her heart.

The pacemaker in his heart kept Dad stuck in security,
but we managed to swim to a nearby shore.

The stranger beside me talked non-stop about his insecurity
and there seems to be no sign of the island of Bermuda.

The lost luggage sign was completely misleading. We gave in
and divided Miguel's muscular thigh between us to keep from starving.

A baby was crying the whole way, as if starving.
I believe myself to be the only survivor.

We were held up in traffic for five days
only to find that the baby was not divine.

Murder is apparently not uncommon on the Orient Express, and the food was less than divine.

—*Megin Jiménez*

3437.

EARLY IN THE MORNING

Improbable, between the new school

And the warning signs, it hangs nearly

Invisible against the post-storm sky.

My first impulse is to photograph it

As if my memory is no longer enough.

Your first spiderweb without a television—

You label it quickly yet I cannot tell

If you recognize its singular beauty or anything

It may represent. You try to grab it but I intercept.

It will be destroyed soon enough and I don't want

The ripped gossamer on our hands. The bus

Drivers are showing the other children. Teachers

Are watching from the window; the secret is up

And the spider can no longer hide in plain sight.

She worked through the night threading with the same

Ignorance I had while you were growing inside of me.

I wish I were still like the spider, oblivious

Of what's looming, walking a few inches

From hands that destroy everything in less

Time than it takes to swat a fly.

—*Jennifer Franklin*

4196.

THE WEATHER IS FINE, AND I AM IMPROVING IT

Last night Fred asked why the house is so messy, his
beautiful small hands shades of cream, pink, and gold
in a howling dark syncopated by the ticking of watches,
our tremendous potential a euphemism for neglected
pargeting. For me, that's better than dancing with rats
or reviving a left-for-dead duckling by popping it into
my bra, where I can feel its tiny eyelids twitch and I
leave the road altogether, crashing into someone else
who recalls starling pâté in the Saint-Rémy market
not as an escape from the real but as reality itself,
with the reward for each of us precisely the same
if you know what I mean. Friends eat, drink, bury
you, and watch a football game torn from the screen
inside a dark bar where two men chalk pool cues away
from the blazing metallic blue of another étang.

—*Ron Horning*

7983.

ALL WERE TAKEN BY SURPRISE

Kirk looked away. "All?"
he asked. Spock nodded.
Kirk heard the thrumming
of the *Enterprise's* engines,
like the blood in his ears;
it had taken him a long time
before he could differentiate
that quiet hum. Even now,
the nearly-silent throb
thrilled him to the core
when he whispered, "Warp
speed!" and one place
became another in a blink.
*Thank god humans can
still blink*, he thought.
He turned back to the great
expanse of whatever had
replaced glass in what they
used to call a windshield.
Cars, he smiled to himself,
remember cars? Mr. Spock
waited for Kirk to speak.
"*All?*" the captain said again.
"The *Surprise* was on us
before we could blink, Jim.
We didn't have a chance."
"Scotty?" "All, Captain—
all were taken by *Surprise*."
Kirk blinked back his tears.

"Warp speed!" he shouted,
savagely. *"Warp speed!"*
His hand on Kirk's forearm,
Spock whispered, "Jim,
it's only us now, only us."
He paused. "I hate to ask,
but can you fly this crate?"

—*James Cummins*

5723.

NO ONE WAS KILLED

None among us who survived is with child.
Omnividence is our sole stratagem,
our one attempt to reorder the mild
neighboring horizon. Still our stars dim,
even the ones most pious and stranded.
What else were we to do? What other small
animals offered us refuge? Our hands
scorned us, our faces; we were unable,
knowing the endurable truth, to die.
If innocence yet exists, we will grow
less with each humid snowfall. We will be
luxuriant in our earthy sorrow,
exiting as if praying to enter.
Death will adjudge us sound, punctiliar.

Death will adjudge us sound, punctiliar,
entropy, yawing, drop us from its nets
like a brisk shimmer of minnows. How far
love must travel to become this clear, this
interesting. We never threw knives or saw
Kirilian photography, and now
so many here brave a vestigial
awareness, a tender penchant for clouds.
Whether or not we appear envious,
each clashes in their rush to be undone.
Nights are wind-spare, ascetic, credulous,

offering the wake of a piebald stone.
One by one we are typecast, reconciled.
None among us who survived is with child.

—*Hailey Leithauser*

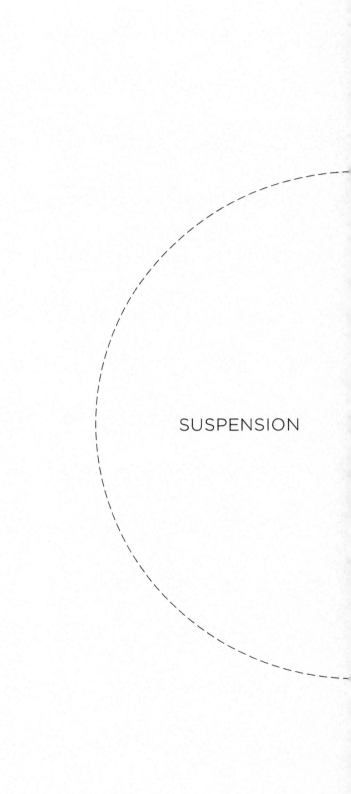

SUSPENSION

1209.

BUSINESS IS DULL ON THE CANAL

Once in a great while, a barge will appear
or wake me in my shack with its whistle,
much like the pitch of Steamboat Willie's,

and I will have to turn the iron wheels
that fill and drain the length of the lock
and hitch the horses to the forward rings,

but other than that, it's just me
and a few ducks that feed along the shore
and the towpath overgrown with grass and chicory.

—*Billy Collins*

6001.

THE COUNTRY IS QUITE LEVEL

The country is quite level
Here. But wet, so wet
The houses sit on stilts.
As do the dead. And
One story up
They measure out
The wind, the tides,
The Mississippi's
Sudden rise.

In this Ninth Ward,
The slightest rain is worrying.

You step
On sun-warmed stones
And miss their sturdiness.
The sun moves higher in the sky.
You never see it rise.
You only see it sink

And see yourself in that.
You watch the flood line
Freshly painted black

and wait.

—*Jamie Stern*

8305.

THE WEATHER IS UNSETTLED

The four of us talk
about first loves.
We admit none
of us married
our first loves.
We defend
our conjugal choices
like a Greek choir, we chant:
"I love my husband, my wife . . ."
but it was not he or she
but someone else
who came before.
We fall silent
betraying our spouses, ourselves.

—*Maria Lisella*

4552.

A GENERAL GLOOM PERVADES THIS COMMUNITY

The willows sag a little deeper.
The hounds jowl a little lower.
The cloud's silver is a plum
that shades each flower in a funk

The lip of the cup is busted.
The leak of each tap is rusted.
The ball's thread is a fray
that turns each pitch into a skunk

A general gloom pervades
with no civility to rescue it
from the dark horizon fast approaching.

—*Dan Vera*

7920.

IT IS BEST TO SUBMIT
AND MAKE THE BEST OF IT

> Mild trauma means mild
> medication; taken, thus, without food,
> I let the morning drowsy—
> light nothing
> like egg yolk, better
> than the lavender flash of signs. Night then,
> this almost now: my ears ring,
> traffic glides over the bridge: matchbox,
> sirens, quiet, sirens,
> matchbox. If you don't
> have anything to say,
> *sit here quieter.* In the morning
> a jackhammer is the bird of prey.
> Against the window, a touch I cannot feel.

> —*Dan Kraines*

7546.

THE ROADS ARE INDIFFERENT

I drove my father to the VA
for a swallow test.
He failed.

He used to be stronger than me.
Taller, better all around.

I took a towel and wiped
his face.
His big farmboy hands,
knobby and translucent,
shook as he clung to his walker
for the long march down
the fluorescent-lighted gauntlet
to the parking lot.

At the funeral
his friends
said I looked just like him.

—Len Joy

6226.

PLEASE INFORM THE MAYOR

      while holiness
      may win access to a better space,
      fervent prayer
      won't help us find a parking place

                    —*Jon Swan*

4830.

THE HEIRS WILL NOT CONSENT

The day I stop wishing for his money—cut myself
From his unwritten will—rub out the rainy-day faces
From the piggybank riches that can only be mine—

Then I'll be alone with my body—my disinherited
Rust—my still-workable bones—
I'll take it for walks—it will be my animal—

Short walks—on a low-numbered city street—
Days before Halloween—when the body
Has to be kept on a short leash—it might run off—

And I'll worry maybe my father—being among the dead—
Will find me—*don't look* I'll say—not even in store windows—
Everything a bare mirror to be stumbled into—

Not even in the jewelry shop at dusk—velvet throats
Stripped of their bling—
What will I have then but passwords—

This one to shut down the account—
This one to read the messages—
This one to not beg favors—of the remembered ones—

Remembered I mean in a codicil—
The dressed-up, walking-by people—
All the others made by the one who made me—

—*Michael Tyrell*

4738.

HARSH LANGUAGE WAS USED

This skull and its stretch
of skin seal in and cook
the matter inside, a gray lump
steaming in its skinny case.

Language had been used
against it. Some words muscled
in, all elbows. Some were solder
still warm from the iron, bone
chips, rubber knobs. A bunch
of moons dragged from their
space.

I can't be alone with these,
so some days I try to split
the case. But by then the words
have dissolved, soap bubbles
that burst into fluid and seep
in, become my matter,
what matters.

—*Gretchen Primack*

6723.

THE ORIGINAL CAN NOT BE FOUND

He said, "The Goth master hammer
slams
Constantine's marble toe."

She said, "Words are always trying to make ruin
instruct us."

He said, "The master of the wall speaks
a simpler language.
Bluestone. Limestone. Shale."

She said, "A body walks through fire
stripped raw."

*O brief alphabet
framed by that stone day.*

—*Patricia Carlin*

6030.

MORE LIGHT IS WANTED ON THE SUBJECT
(for H. Edelheit, 1920–1981)

When I hear the song of the heart-sized frogs
crooning from a diminished choir,
I remember Dr. E betrayed by malevolent cells
how he told me he despised dissecting frogs
in biology class.
Later, he showed me his drawings of tadpoles.

Today in the meadow, hoarse voices in a ring
call for the promise of morning, their summoner.
A man I almost recognize sketches the gingko tree
in a fog of stirred air. I think I see him in his chair,
tilted forward, and long for his silences,
how they prodded me to speak.

—*Colette Inez*

997.

IT IS SUPPOSED THE BOAT IS DETAINED BY FOG

Though this rumor, for it is nothing more or less,
a collective certainty that the Atlantic has not claimed
another ship on a milk-white night, relies solely on hope,
hence is too much to bear—no one can see, lighthouse
beam diffuse, fog horn blasts muffled in the seeded air.
                    I slip down
to the water's edge, eyes coated in white muck,
feeling my way one foot at a time, arms raised in defense
against the unseen, I lift my skirts, wade in to my waist;
                    I will wait here.

—Deborah McAlister

3078.

EVERY THING HERE LOOKS VERY DISMAL

But if there were rabbits, clustered beneath the chestnut trees, uncanny in twilight.
If there were ancient wooden houses, and kitchen gardens stretching toward the
tracks, with knobby cabbages or trellises of beans that cast long shadows as the
train clattered by. If women moved slowly back and forth, scattering feed from
battered pails, if chickens flustered up clucking, pecking, with their curious hitch
gait. If men came from the barns in muddy boots, bulky sweaters tucked into their
overalls, and scraped their boots, entered their kitchens, shut their blue doors.

If night came down as we gazed out the window, if fields folded themselves like
cloaks and sank into sleep. If we sank into sleep. And if we rode on the train as
summer passed, then autumn, as it carried us into the mountains, till we came to
a river so cold it burned. If we crossed it asleep on stepping stones, flapping our
gawky wings.

                        —*Ann Fisher-Wirth*

2268.

I SHALL TAKE A DIFFERENT COURSE

In the interest of full disclosure
I find myself lightheaded, results
of motion sickness, reading one

required chapter after another,
blood sugar, and what's the German
word for when a person asks

what the German word is for some
such sensation: *That*. In the interest
of full disclosure I am edging

toward the train's open window
only partially for the fresh air
it invites and also, simultaneously

calculating the damage a fall at this
speed would perform. There are
numerous ways to live. I shall take

a different course as nothing much
is portended this way, not encounters
with raccoons near a civic stream

or the rabbits on the green suburban
median strip witnessed from this train
window travelling between a place

of culture, adequate culinary experiences,
and another known for taking in
the mountain air. Nothing works magic.

I believe that is the point, that at some
point, if patient, I will arrive somewhere
to pass time or recoup from previous

attempts to recover from the time
remaining. I will change. I will drink
a daily quota of water, half my given

body weight, the dark circles disappear.
Quit cigarettes. Pay off the card with
the highest interest rate first. I should

start over, I mean again closing my eyes
for a designated amount of breathing.
Understand what ails may only be

this view I selected, known colloquially
as the sky is overcast and rain probable.
Known technically as tomorrow.

All portents are unlucky because
I will it. I repeat facts. Either it is day
or night out any window. Either there

is sleep or the trying to sleep. I prefer
to think there is tomorrow for thinking
it can be otherwise, thinking soon

this blur of forests will be restored
mystery, owls, moss and so on.
In the interest of full disclosure I find

it fit to permanently sit this one out,
today is already finished, misremembered
how an honorable man from historical

fiction mistakes his intended destination
for wherever he was at any given breath.
That's me. Pencils down. I'm finished.

—*Brett Fletcher Lauer*

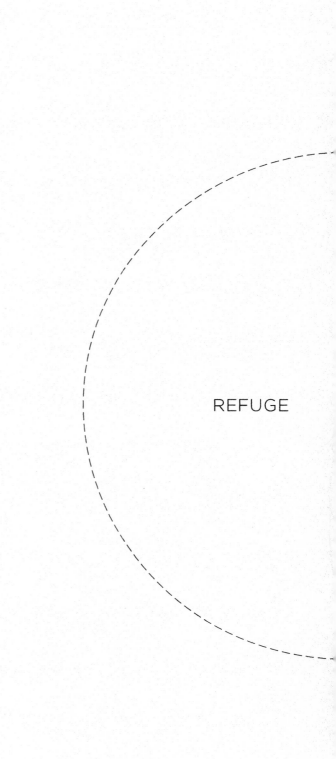

REFUGE

8127.

I AM IN TROUBLE, AND NEED ASSISTANCE

When I lived in Brazil, I often dined in a restaurant with a tree-shaded courtyard. One night in November, which is to say, summer, my friend Julio appeared beside my table, tall lovely gay Julio with lashes long as a giraffe's. He slid the black leather dessert menu out of my fingers. *Look up, Betchy*—that's how they said my name in that country—*Betchy, look up.* I looked up into the jabucabeira tree, which I had frequently admired, and saw its trunk and limbs were studded with fruit. Heavy black fruit, scrotal, was growing right out of the branches, which were drooping now just out of reach. And this is the part where Julio smiles. *Calma, Betchy, calma.* He pulls a branch down to where I sit in my embroidered skirt. Without having to shift in my chair, without even uncrossing my legs—it's that easy—merely by raising my arm, I grasp a fruit and, like unscrewing a lightbulb, release it into my dominion.

Friends appearing by my side. Ripe fruit dangling overhead. Unpremeditated bliss. Is it clear to you now, at last, and for good? That's the type of assistance I need.

—Beth Ann Fennelly

4839.

HELP HAS BEEN OBTAINED

No thanks to you.

—*Joe Zendarski*

56.

GOOD NEWS! THE HARBOR IS IN SIGHT

though men appear as flies and the village
flimsy toys a child-god's whim it's been
years since I waved *we may never meet*
again we are bound for miniature ponies black
volcanoes and ice! as in granite dreams will I
still know (salt-crusted) you will you
shrink back or hesitate or lie let's not
pretend life is beautiful but strain towards
familiar strange faces gathered to meet us

—*Claudia Burbank*

3079.

THINGS DO NOT LOOK AS DISMAL AS THEY DID

for the Waccamaw fatmucket and Ozark hellbender
moved a step closer to protection as endangered, along with the
Alabama map turtle, Avernus cave beetle,

Blueridge springfly & Bicknell's thrush,
Cape Fear spatterdock & Christ's paintbrush,
Dakota skipper & dusky tree vole,

Egg-mimic darter & elfin-woods warbler,
Fuzzy pigtoe & frecklebelly madtom,
Georgia blind salamander, Gulf Hammock dwarf siren,

Harper's heartleaf & Hirst Brothers' panic grass,
Ichetucknee siltsnail & impressed-nerved sedge,
Jackson Prairie crayfish, Jefferson County crayfish,

Kentucky glade cress & knobby rams-horn,
Large-flowered Barbara's buttons & Linda's roadside-skipper,
Mojave fringe-toed lizard & Miami blue butterfly,

Narrowleaf naiad, New England cottontail,
Overlooked cave beetle, oceanic Hawaiian damselfly,
Pacific walrus, peppered shiner, Pagosa skyrocket, purple

            lilliput, & thin-wall
Quillwort,
Rabbitsfoot, Raven's seedbox, rivergrass & rayed creekshell,

Soothsayer cave beetle, spectaclecase pearly mussel,
Tacoma pocket gopher, Tallapoosa orb, Texas trillium &
        Tehama chaparral,

Umbilicate pebblesnail,
Vandenberg monkeyflower,
Western fanshell & whorled sunflower,

Xantus's murrelet,
Yellow-billed loon, Yazoo crayfish &
Zuni bluehead sucker:

    all might be saved.

                    —*Barbara Ungar*

7237.

THE RAIN IS OVER, APPARENTLY

Wild west of here, where snow
is more often rain

and more often still the bluest skies
you'd never seen,

there are paid professionals
monitoring the climate situation.

We don't change, but there's proof
that some things do, the clouds

a pleasant bloat
all these states later, like we haven't known

for days, not since we last
licked each other's wounds,

drowning out the violence
with violence, making our own

scars with bits of broken anything
closer and closer

to the heart, beating
whatever's beating us

to the punch, no matter
the hour, whatever the weather.

—*Lynn Melnick*

4453.

THE FUNERAL WAS LARGELY ATTENDED
"Our Family of Sorrow at the Tomb," Caravaggio 1603-04

As a single
figure this would appear
as grotesquely
overdressed as a provincial
Indian deity
or a *menina*. But this
is neither
a single figure nor one of those
strange paintings
composed of vegetables
or fruit. This is
a pietá of people. From
Lazarus's
sister's palm, the perfume
of death first blooms.
Here, it bursts and falls like confetti
on the five
individuals; that
opened hand, those
lowered faces. If standing here
that night, we
wouldn't be simply
in the garden,
but in the grave. The man bent
over like John
is either Nicodemus
or Joseph of
Arimathea. As they must begin

to lower him now,
he turns to let us know
that it is time
for them to hand him down to us.

—*Scott Hightower*

6487.

PLEASE GIVE ME THE NAME OF

The murder of García Lorca
was ordered by one man
and carried out by another
who volunteered to join
the great crusade of their people
to purify its blood
and keep their names forever
inscribed in their people's book.

Now the historians
ferret out their names
and reveal them both to the world.
It is infamy's reward.

Revile them without their names.
Obliterate both names.

—*Barry Goldensohn*

6156.

LIVES IN GREAT MAGNIFICENCE

were lost. Heaven's legions, in the millions,
speared, lanced each other, only to heal back
again to hack and hurt, until Satan's army
cheats. A-bombs and mustard gas not yet imagined,
even by Milton, the rebels cannot see
they are doomed to lose. Yet,
in all this mayhem on the plains

of heaven, where are the female angels?
Are there Amazon brigades
on both sides, led by Penthesilea
and Hippolyta? Medieval scholars believed
angels to be genderless, therefore male,
unaware that genderless bees

are female. Maybe there are no female angels,
but how could there be heaven without them?
No wonder there came war and envy.
Erased from the giant star directory,
all those fallen ones
beyond the sky, Eden lost, the sons
of God mating with the daughters of men.

—*Stuart Bartow*

7671.

IT IS NO SECRET HERE

Dirt, wrote a British anthropologist,
is matter out of place. Drop a grape
from bowl to table and we call it *dirty.*
Drop a grape to the floor and it is *trash.*
Bowl, table: these are ordering agents,
ways to tell the functional from fallen.

Skin, tendon: these are ordering agents.

You want to kiss my mouth, but not
 the teeth inside my mouth. You want
to hold my hand, but not the blood
within that hand. There is a truth
in you, but it won't be the dirty truth
until it tumbles into the air between
us. In this city, there is always
a long walk home in 7 a.m. light,
high heels stabbing the subway grates.
A walk home past gutters littered
with the non sequitur of chicken bones,
wings that once held a dream of flight.

—*Sandra Beasley*

7647.

THE CARGO IS SAVED

A turnbuckle clangs
against a flagpole.
Rope chafes
cleats and winches.
Bowed planks creak
in the slow swell.
Slow trough.

Wind.
Seagulls
hang like kites.
Is the wind heard
because motionless wings
offer resistance?
The surf whispers its sleeping spell
home home
over the open eyes of sailors.

Sounds of metal
on metal, wood
on wood, water
and water and
water. "Listen,"
we say, what's
easiest to say,
"It's so silent."

—*Martin Jude Farawell*

1644.

THERE ARE FLYING CLOUDS
OF DOUBTFUL IMPORT

The world
is opposed
to you.

Ariel blows.

Taxed and waged,
too high, too low.

You must
choose
between
good company
and good air.

Leaves
don't obey.

You must
obey
but your hair
flies

in the face
of gravity,
his sky.

—*Anja Konig*

1878.

IT IS COMPLETE

and finally done
I turn away from

loose threads and
fingerprints

worms of bindweed
in the loam

maintenance
and entropy

rock weathering
down

—*Tim Cresswell*

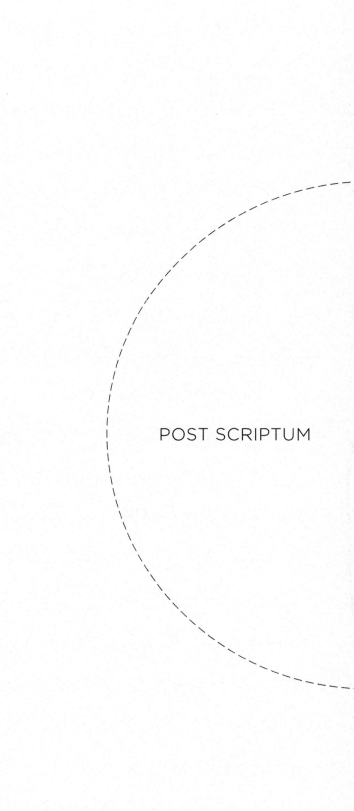

POST SCRIPTUM

431.

THE ENTERPRISE IS ABANDONED

I'm not a fool, I knew from the beginning
what couldn't happen. What couldn't happen

didn't. *The enterprise is abandoned.*

But half our life is
dreams, delirium, everything that underlies

that feeds

that keeps alive the illusion of sanity, semi-
sanity, we allow

others to see. The half of me that feeds the rest

is in mourning. Mourns. Each time we must
mourn, we fear this is the final mourning, this time

mourning never will lift. A friend said when a lover

dies, it takes
two years. Then it lifts.

Inside those two years, you punish

not only the world,
but yourself.

At seventy-two, the future is what I mourn.

Since college I've never forgotten Masha
in *The Seagull* saying *I am in mourning for my life.*

She wears only black, she treats others with

fierce solicitude
and sudden punishment.

The enterprise is abandoned. And not.

—*Frank Bidart*

DESIRÉE ALVAREZ's first collection, *Devil's Paintbrush*, won the 2015 May Sarton New Hampshire Poetry Prize from Bauhan Publishing. Her poems have appeared in *Poetry, Boston Review, The Iowa Review,* and *Prairie Schooner.* Fellowships include Yaddo and Poets House. She is also a visual artist who exhibits widely. Awards include Willard L. Metcalf Award from the American Academy of Arts and Letters. She teaches at CUNY, The Juilliard School, and Artists Space.

ANN ASPELL is a book designer and editor, a co-founder of Chapiteau Press, and a writing instructor at Community College of Vermont. Her poems have appeared in journals such as *Hunger Mountain, Poetry International,* and *Magma.*

STUART BARTOW's most recent book of poems, *Einstein's Lawn*, is published by Dos Madres Press. He teaches writing and literature at SUNY Adirondack, where he directs the college's Writers Project. His book of lyric essays, *Teaching Trout to Talk: the Zen of Small Stream Fly Fishing*, won this year's Adirondack Center for Writing non-fiction award. He lives in Salem, New York, where he likes to fish and hike.

HARRY BAULD was chosen by Matthew Dickman for inclusion in *Best New Poets 2012* and won the *New Millennium Writings* Poetry Prize and the Milton Kessler 2015 Award from Harpur Palate. His work has appeared in *Nimrod, Southern Poetry Review, The Southeast Review, Verse Daily,* and *Ruminate,* among others. He teaches in the Bronx.

SANDRA BEASLEY is the author of three poetry collections—*Count the Waves, I Was the Jukebox,* and *Theories of Falling*—and a memoir, *Don't Kill the Birthday Girl: Tales from an Allergic Life.* Honors for her work include a 2015 NEA fellowship, the Center for Book Arts Chapbook Prize, and two DC Commission on the Arts and Humanities fellowships. She lives in Washington, DC, and teaches with the University of Tampa low-residency MFA program.

FRANK BIDART is the author of nine books of poems. His collected works *Half-light: Collected Poems 1965–2016* is forthcoming from FSG (April 2017). He has won many prizes, including the Wallace Stevens Award, the 2007 Bollingen Prize for American Poetry, and the National Book Critics Circle Award. He teaches at Wellesley College and lives in Cambridge, Massachusetts.

CHIP BROWN is the author of two non-fiction books, and has published articles in more than forty national magazines including *National Geographic, Vogue, Esquire, Outside, Vanity Fair, The New Yorker,* and *The New York Times Magazine* where he is a contributing writer. He lives in New York with Kate Betts, his wife of twenty years, and their two children, Oliver and India.

CLAUDIA BURBANK's honors include the Maureen Egen Writers Exchange Award from Poets & Writers, two Fellowships from the New Jersey Arts Council, the Inkwell Prize, *Best New Poets 2013,* and a Jentel Artist Residency Fellowship. Her prose and poetry have been published in *Subtropics, The Antioch Review, The Literary Review, Prairie Schooner,* and *upstreet,* among other journals.

PATRICIA CARLIN's new poetry collection *Second Nature* is forthcoming from Marsh Hawk Press. Previous books include *Quantum Jitters* and *Original Green* (poems), and *Shakespeare's Mortal Men* (prose). Her work has appeared widely in journals and anthologies such as *Verse, Boulevard, POOL, Pleiades, McSweeney's Internet Tendency, American Letters & Commentary, The Manhattan Review,* and *BOMB.* She teaches at The New School and co-edits the poetry journal *Barrow Street.*

J. GERARD CHALMERS is a New York writer with an MFA from Columbia University. She has published poems, reviews, and social commentary in many literary publications such as *Bellevue Literary Review, Barrow Street, New Millennium Writings, Fogged Clarity, The Naugatuck River Review,* and the *Kenyon Review* (online) and was nominated for the 2014 anthology, *Best New Poets.* She is currently writing a book of poetry called "Scorpion Love" about Picasso's mistress, the artist Dora Maar.

132

BILLY COLLINS is the author of eleven collections of poetry. As Poet Laureate of the United States from 2001 to 2003, he founded Poetry 180, a program designed to interest high school students in poetry. He is a Distinguished Professor of English at Lehman College of the City University of New York. His latest book is *The Rain in Portugal*.

TIM CRESSWELL is a geographer and poet. He is the author of *Soil* (Penned in the Margins, 2013) and *Fence* (Penned in the Margins, 2015). His poems are widely published in magazines including *Poetry Wales*, *The Rialto*, *Cider Press Review*, *Riddlefence*, *Magma*, and *The Moth*. He is Dean of Faculty and Vice President for Academic Affairs at Trinity College, Hartford and lives in West Hartford, Connecticut, with his family.

LAURA CRONK is a poet and essayist. She is the author of *Having Been an Accomplice* from Persea Books and directs the Summer Writers Colony and other programs for writers at The New School.

JAMES CUMMINS lives in Cincinnati. His most recent book is *Still Some Cake* (Carnegie Mellon, 2012).

DENISE DUHAMEL's book of poetry *Blowout* (University of Pittsburgh Press, 2013) was a finalist for the National Book Critics Circle Award. Her other titles include *Ka-Ching!* (Pittsburgh, 2009), *Two and Two* (Pittsburgh, 2005), *Queen for a Day: Selected and New Poems* (Pittsburgh, 2001), *The Star-Spangled Banner* (winner of the Crab Orchard Award, SIU Press, 1999), and *Kinky* (Orchises Press, 1997). Duhamel is a professor at Florida International University in Miami.

HUANG FAN is the author of two novels and three collections of poetry, most recently *Huang Fan: 10 Years of Poetry*. His honors include the Fangcao Poetry Prize, the Jinling Literary Prize, and fellowships from Cross-Strait Writers Exchange, University of Göttingen, and the Henry Luce Foundation. He lives in Nanjing where he teaches literature at Nanjing University of Science and Technology.

MARTIN JUDE FARAWELL is the author of a chapbook *Genesis: A Sequence of Poems*, and his work has appeared in a variety of journals and anthologies. His plays have been performed Off-Off-Broadway and by regional, college, community, and international theaters from South Africa to Los Angeles. A graduate of New York University's Creative Writing Program, he directs the Geraldine R. Dodge Poetry Festival.

BETH ANN FENNELLY directs the MFA Program at Ole Miss where she was named Outstanding Teacher of the Year. She's won grants from the NEA, United States Artists, and a Fulbright to Brazil. Fennelly has published three books of poetry and one of nonfiction, all with W. W. Norton. Her most recent is *The Tilted World*, a novel co-authored with her husband, Tom Franklin. They live in Oxford with their three children.

ANN FISHER-WIRTH's fourth book of poems, *Dream Cabinet*, was published by Wings Press in 2012. She is coeditor of *Ecopoetry Anthology*, (Trinity University Press, 2013) and is currently collaborating on a book project with the acclaimed Mississippi photographer Maude Schuyler Clay. The recipient of numerous awards and prizes, she is a 2015–2018 Fellow of the Black Earth Institute, an international think tank. She teaches at the University of Mississippi.

EMILY FRAGOS is the recipient of a Guggenheim Fellowship in Poetry, a Literature Award from the American Academy of Arts & Letters, and the 2015 Witter Bynner Prize from the Library of Congress. She has published two books of poetry, *Hostage* (2011) and *Little Savage* (2004), and edited five anthologies for the Everyman's Pocket Library. Emily Fragos is a native New Yorker who teaches at NYU and Columbia University.

JENNIFER FRANKLIN has degrees from Brown and Columbia. Her collection, *Looming*, won the fourteenth Editor's Prize from Elixir Press. Her work has appeared in *Boston Review*, *Gettysburg Review*, *Guernica*, *The Nation*, *New England Review*, *The Paris Review*, "Poem-a-Day" on poets.org, *Poetry Daily*, and *Verse Daily*. Franklin is co-editor of Slapering Hol Press, the small press imprint of The Hudson Valley Writers' Center. She teaches at HVWC and lives in New York City.

GREGG FRIEDBERG is the author of *The Best Seat Not in the House* (Main Street Rag, 2010), a poem sequence, and *Would You Be Made Whole?* (Alrich Press, 2015), a collection of "unruly sonnets." He prefers writing poem sequences: loosely narrative, a matrix of themes considered from varying perspective, and divides his time between Guanajuato, Mexico, and Upper Sandusky, Ohio.

BARRY GOLDENSOHN has taught in many schools, including Goddard in the '60s and '70s, the Writers' Workshop at Iowa, Hampshire College, and Skidmore College. His poem included in this anthology appears in his seventh collection of poems, a book dealing with politics as seen by a non-political man. He is married to the poet and scholar Lorrie Goldensohn.

MICHAEL GOTTLIEB is the author of nineteen books. His latest, *What We Do: Essays for Poets*, has just been published by Chax Press. He is also the author of *Memoir and Essay*, the authoritative recounting of the rise of Language poetry. A number of his poems have been adopted for the stage, including his 9/11 poem, *The Dust*, which was performed at the Poetry Subject at St. Marks on the tenth anniversary of the attacks.

After teaching at Goucher College, LEE GOULD retired to the Hudson Valley where she continues to teach and write. Her poems, essays and reviews have appeared in *Salmagundi*, *The Berkshire Review*, *Passager*, and other journals and in anthologies including *A Slant of Light: Contemporary Women Writers of the Hudson Valley*. Her chapbook *Weeds* was published by Finishing Line Press in 2010.

SONJA GRECKOL is a Canadian poet. *Skein of Days* (Pedlar Press, 2014) deploys newspaper and magazine headings and subheads from Greckol's own place and time, with flashes of popular song titles, particles of scientific lexicon, and a poetic record of Canadian award-winning poetry. *Gravity Matters* (Inanna Press, 2009), her first book, tracks oft-opposing forces of "gravity and flight." Her poems have appeared in a variety of Canadian journals.

MONICA A. HAND is the author of *me and Nina* (Alice James Books, 2012). Her poems have been published in *Pleiades*, *Oxford American*, *Spoon River Poetry*

Review, Black Renaissance Noire, The Sow's Ear, and *Drunken Boat.* She has an MFA in Poetry and Poetry in Translation from Drew University, and currently, she is a PhD candidate in Poetry at the University of Missouri-Columbia.

SCOTT HIGHTOWER is the author of four books of poetry in the US and *Hontanares,* a bilingual collection (Spanish and English) published by Devenir, Madrid. His third book won the 2004 Hayden Carruth Award. Hightower's translations from Spanish have garnered him a prestigious Barnstone Translation Prize. When not teaching as adjunct faculty at NYU, the Gallatin School, he sojourns in Spain.

NORBERT HIRSCHHORN is a public health physician, commended by President Bill Clinton as an "American Health Hero." He lives in London. He has published four collections, the most recent, *To Sing Away the Darkest Days: Poems Re-imagined from Yiddish Folksongs* (Holland Park Press, London, 2013). His poems have appeared in numerous US/UK publications, several as prize-winning. See his website, www.bertzpoet.com.

EVA HOOKER is Professor of English and Writer in Residence at Saint Mary's College, Notre Dame, Indiana. Her latest collection is *Godwit* (3: A Taos Press, 2016). Her *Notes for Survival in the Wilderness* (2013) was published by Chapiteau Press, which also published *The Winter Keeper,* a hand-bound chapbook, a finalist for the Minnesota Book Award in poetry. Her poems have recently appeared in *The New England Review, Agni, The Harvard Review,* and *Best New Poets.*

RON HORNING lives and works in Beacon, New York. His poems and translations have appeared in *The New Yorker, Vanitas, Gerry Mulligan, Sal Mimeo, Insurance,* and *The Hat,* and he has written prose reports for *Aperture, The Village Voice, LA Weekly, index,* and *The Brooklyn Rail.* In 2014, Color Treasury published a group of three poems entitled *From Philip Drunk to Philip Sober.*

BERGEN HUTAFF is a former member of the Chicago Board of Trade. Her work has appeared in *Barrow Street* and she lives in New York City.

COLETTE INEZ has authored eleven poetry collections, most recently *The Luba Poems* (Red Hen Press, 2015). She has received fellowships from the Guggenheim and Rockefeller Foundations and won NEA grants and Pushcart prizes. She taught at Cornell, Bucknell, and other universities before joining the faculty of Columbia University's Undergraduate Writing Program. Her memoir *The Secret of M. Dulong* was published by University of Wisconsin Press. She was born in Belgium and resides in New York with her husband of fifty-one years.

MEGIN JIMÉNEZ was born in Mérida, Venezuela, and grew up in Denver. Her work has appeared in *Barrow Street, Denver Quarterly, La Petite Zine, LIT, NOO Journal,* and *Sentence,* among other journals. She is a graduate of The New School Writing Program and co-hosted Monday Night Poetry at KGB Bar for many years. She works as a translator and lives in Leiden, the Netherlands.

BETH BARUCH JOSELOW is the author of a dozen books and chapbooks of poems, as well as plays, essays, short stories, and books on divorce and creative writing. During her tenure teaching writing at the Corcoran College of Art in Washington, DC, she collaborated with artists in the United States and Ukraine to create prints and artists' books. She now works as a counselor in Lewes, Delaware.

LEN JOY lives in Evanston, Illinois. Recent work has appeared in *FWRICTION: Review, The Journal of Compressed Creative Arts, Johnny America, Specter Magazine, Washington Pastime, Hobart, Annalemma,* and *Pindeldyboz.* His novel, *American Past Time,* about a minor league baseball player whose life unravels after he fails to make it to the major leagues, was published by Hark! New Era Publishing in April 2014. He is currently working on the sequel.

DAVID M. KATZ is the author of three books of poems: *Stanzas on Oz* (Dos Madres Press), *Claims of Home* (Dos Madres Press), and *The Warrior in the Forest* (House of Keys Press). His poems have appeared in *Poetry, The New Criterion, The Paris Review, PN Review, The Raintown Review, Alabama Literary Review,* and *Southwest Review.* He lives in New York City, where he works as a financial journalist.

ANJA KONIG grew up in the German language and now writes in English. Her first chapbook *Advice for an Only Child* is out from Flipped Eye Publishing. Its advantages are 1) it is very cheap, 2) it is very short.

DAN KRAINES's poetry has appeared in *The Journal, Saint Ann's Review, Salmagundi,* and elsewhere. He writes and teaches at the University of Rochester, where he is a PhD student and Slattery Fellow. He holds an MFA in poetry from Boston University and an interdisciplinary MA in modernism from NYU. He has taught at Skidmore College and is the graduate director of the Plutzik Reading Series and an editor for *Two Peach.*

QUINN LATIMER is an American poet, critic, and editor based in Athens, Greece. She is the author of *Rumored Animals* (2012) and *Sarah Lucas: Describe This Distance* (2013), which explores the work of Lucas as well as shame, palindromes, passivity, fertility statuary, Napoleon, Artaud, and Sontag. A regular contributor to *Artforum* and a contributing editor to *frieze,* Latimer is currently Editor-in-Chief of Publications for *documenta 14.*

BRETT FLETCHER LAUER is the author of the memoir *Fake Missed Connections: Divorce, Online Dating, and Other Failures* (Soft Skull, 2016) and the book of poems *A Hotel in Belgium* (Four Way Books, 2014). He is the deputy director of the Poetry Society of America and the poetry editor for *A Public Space.*

DAVID LEHMAN is a poet, writer, and editor. His most recent books are *Sinatra's Century: One Hundred Notes on the Man and His World* (HarperCollins, 2015) and *New and Selected Poems* (Scribner Poetry, 2013). He is the editor of *The Oxford Book of American Poetry* and the series editor of *The Best American Poetry,* the annual anthology that he initiated in 1988. He teaches in the New School Writing Program in New York City.

HAILEY LEITHAUSER is the author of *Swoop* (Graywolf, 2013) which won the Poetry Foundation's Emily Dickinson First Book Award, the Towson Prize for Literature, and was a finalist for the Kate Tufts First Book Award. She has new work in *Agni, Field, The Gettysburg Review, Poetry,* and *The Yale Review,* and has appeared in three editions of *The Best American Poetry.*

MARIA LISELLA is the author of a poetry collection, *Thieves in the Family* (NYQ Books), and two chapbooks, *Amore on Hope Street* (Finishing Line Press) and *Two Naked Feet* (Poets Wear Prada). She co-curates the Italian American Writers Association readings, is a charter member of brevitas, and is the newest Queens Poet Laureate 2015–2018. She is an award-winning travel writer and editor.

STEPHEN MASSIMILLA's co-authored book, *Cooking with the Muse,* is just out from Tupelo Press. He received an SFASU Press Prize for *The Plague Doctor in His Hull-Shaped Hat;* the Bordighera Poetry Prize for *Forty Floors from Yesterday* (CUNY); the Grolier Poetry Prize for *Later on Aiaia;* a Van Renssalaer Award, selected by Kenneth Koch; and others. He holds an MFA and a PhD from Columbia University and teaches at Columbia University and the New School.

DEBORAH MCALISTER is a poet and editor and lifelong New Yorker. She is one of a team of editors for *Tupelo Quarterly* (TQ) an online journal associated with Tupelo Press. She is also an active trustee at The Lark, a groundbreaking incubator of new plays. Her poem "Training for Iraq" was published in the *Asheville Poetry Review.* Others have appeared in a variety of now defunct online journals, including *Fling Quarterly.* She is at work on a manuscript called "Calibration."

LYNN MELNICK is author of *If I Should Say I Have Hope* (YesYes Books, 2012) and co-editor, with Brett Fletcher Lauer, of *Please Excuse This Poem: 100 New Poets for the Next Generation* (Viking, 2015). She teaches at 92Y in New York City and is the social media & outreach director for VIDA: Women in Literary Arts.

GRETCHEN PRIMACK is the author of two poetry collections, *Doris' Red Spaces* (Mayapple Press, 2014) and *Kind* (Post-Traumatic Press, 2013). Her poems have appeared in the *Paris Review, Prairie Schooner, Field, Poet Lore, Ploughshares,* and other journals. Also an animal advocate, she co-wrote the memoir *The Lucky Ones: My Passionate Fight for Farm Animals* (Penguin Avery, 2012). www.gretchenprimack.com.

ANNA RABINOWITZ's fifth volume of poetry is *Words on the Street*, which appeared from Tupelo Press in 2016. Earlier volumes are *At the Site of Inside Out, Darkling, The Wanton Sublime,* and *Present Tense.* She has written librettos for *Darkling* and *The Wanton Sublime,* the former as a chamber opera and the latter as a monodrama for a mezzo-soprano. Both operas have been performed here and abroad.

JIMMY ROBERTS is a theater composer, pianist, and poet. His show, *I Love You, You're Perfect, Now Change,* became the second-longest-running Off-Broadway musical ever, and his next one, *The Thing About Men,* was voted "Outstanding New Musical of 2003/2004" by the New York Outer Critics Circle. His poems have appeared often in *The New York Times* as well as *Möbius, the Poetry Magazine.*

MARGARET ROSS is the author of *A Timeshare* (Omnidawn, 2015). Her poems and translations appear in *A Public Space, Boston Review, Conjunctions,* and *Fence.* She was a 2013 Fulbright Fellow in Nanjing and is currently a Stegner Fellow. She and Huang Fan received the Henry Luce Foundation Chinese Poetry and Translation Fellowship and are currently completing a manuscript of his poems in translation.

JO SARZOTTI's book, *Mother Desert,* won the Bakeless Prize selected by Carl Phillips and was published in 2012 by Graywolf Press. Her work has appeared in *Denver Quarterly, The Alaska Quarterly, North American Review, Borderlands,* and *Tupelo Quarterly.* Her poem "Horse Latitudes" is included in the anthology *Poem-a-Day: 365 Poems for Every Occasion* (Abrams Books, 2015). She lives in New York City where she directs the Liberal Arts Department at The Juilliard School.

GAIL SEGAL is a poet and a filmmaker. Her most recent collection of poems, *The Discreet Charm of Prime Numbers,* was published in 2013 by Finishing Line Press. Her most recent film, *Filigrane,* was awarded the Best Short Foreign Language Film at the St. Tropez/Nice International Film Festival. She teaches in the Graduate Division of Film and Television at NYU's Tisch School of the Arts.

ANN SETTEL's work includes her recent poetry collection *Quilt* (The Troy Book Makers, 2016) and poems in *The Western Humanities Review*, *Poet Lore*, and *Naugatuck River Review*. She lives in New York City.

JAMES SHERRY is the author of twelve books of poetry and prose, most recently *Oops! Environmental Poetics*. *Entangled Bank* is forthcoming from Chax Press in the fall of 2016. He is the editor of Roof Books and founder of the Segue Foundation, in New York City.

JAMIE STERN's poetry collection, *Chasing Steam*, was published in 2013 (Virtual Artists Collective). Her poem "Posted" appears in *Pushing the Envelope: Epistolary Poems* (Lamar University Press, 2015). An attorney, Jamie is the co-publisher of six poetry anthologies in honor of Marie Ponsot, *Still Against War*, editions I through VI. Jamie is a member of the board of Poets House, a New York City literary center and poetry library.

RICHARD STULL was born in Mount Gilead, Ohio. He has had a residency at Yaddo and has been awarded an Ingram Merrill Foundation grant. He is the author of several chapbooks, including *Adoration of the Golden Calf*, *A Walk With Jane*, *Drugged Like Mirrors*, and *Canal*. He presently lives in Newburgh, New York, with Karen Cissel and the beagle Jack Sprat.

JULIE SUAREZ lives in Oneonta with her husband, David Hayes, and teaches at Hartwick College. In her small but exuberant garden she grows lilies taller than herself and finds the seeds of many of her poems. Bright Hill Press published her chapbook *It Does Not* in 2006.

JON SWAN is the author of three published collections of poems. *New and Selected Poems* can be found on his website: jonswanpoems. He and his wife live in Yarmouth, Maine.

ABIGAIL THOMAS's most recent book is *What Comes Next and How to Like It*, a memoir.

MICHAEL TYRELL is the author of the poetry collection *The Wanted* (National Poetry Review, 2012), and coeditor, with Julia Spicher Kasdorf, of *Broken Land: Poems of Brooklyn* (NYU, 2007). His poems have appeared in many magazines and anthologies, including *The Best American Poetry 2015*, edited by Sherman Alexie. He teaches writing in New York University's Tisch School of the Arts.

BARBARA UNGAR has published four books of poetry, most recently *Immortal Medusa* (The Word Works, 2015), which won the Adirondack Center for Writing Poetry Award, and *Charlotte Brontë, You Ruined My Life* (The Word Works, 2011). *The Origin of the Milky Way* (Gival Press, 2007) won the Gival Prize, an Independent Publishers silver medal, and a Hoffer award. A professor of English at the College of Saint Rose in Albany, New York, she teaches literature and creative writing. Please see barbaraungar.net.

DAN VERA is a writer, editor, and literary historian living in Washington, DC. His last poetry collection, *Speaking Wiri Wiri*, won the Letras Latinas/Red Hen Poetry Prize. His poetry appears in various journals, anthologies, and university curricula. He co-curates the literary history site *DC Writers' Homes*, and chairs the board of Split This Rock Poetry. LatinoStories.com named him a "New" Latino Author to Watch (and Read).

ABIGAIL WENDER's work has appeared or is forthcoming in the *Cortland Review*, *Epiphany*, *Guernica / A Magazine of Art & Politics*, *The Massachusetts Review*, *New Orleans Review*, and other journals. Her translations appear in *Tupelo Quarterly 1* and *New Haven Review*. She holds an MFA from Warren Wilson College, and lives and teaches in New York City.

CATHERINE WOODARD's collection *Opening the Mouth of the Dead* is forthcoming from lone goose press. A poet and former journalist, she helped return "Poetry in Motion" to the NYC subways and is on the board of the Poetry Society of America. Her poems have appeared in literary journals and CNN online. She writes and plays basketball in New York City.

ERICA WRIGHT is the author of the poetry collection *Instructions for Killing the Jackal*. She is the poetry editor at *Guernica* as well as an editorial board member for Alice James Books. Her latest novel is *The Granite Moth*.

JOE ZENDARSKI is traveling the road of excess in search of the palace of wisdom. He has worked as a barista, busboy, carpenter, construction manager, day laborer, dog walker, landscaper, library aid, mason, and print shop manager. He currently teaches writing at the University of Mississippi.

146

Helen Klein Ross is a poet and novelist whose work has appeared in *The New Yorker*, *The New York Times*, *Salmagundi*, and *The Iowa Review* where it won the 2014 Iowa Review award in poetry. Her found poem "How to Furnish an American House" received commendation in 2012 from the Poetry Society in London. Her latest novel is *What Was Mine* (Simon & Schuster / Gallery, 2016). She lives with her husband in New York City and Salisbury, CT.

CPSIA information can be obtained at www.ICGtesting.com
Printed in the USA
BVOW04s2024071016

464499BV00002B/3/P